Sir Francis Drake

Printed in China

9 8 7 6 5 4 3 2 1
Digit on the right indicates the number of this printing

Designed by: Ryan Hayes
Typography: Baskerville Book and Phaeton

Published by Pirate & Maritime Research Society
12 S. Castillo Drive, St. Augustine, FL 32084

Visit www.patcroce.com or www.thepiratemuseum.com

Sir Francis Drake

by Pat Croce   illustrated by Tristan Elwell

FRANCIS DRAKE was only 28 years old and on his first trading expedition to the New World. As a captain of a small 6-gun ship called *Judith*, he was part of a squadron under the command of his cousin John Hawkins.

In the middle of the journey, Hawkins' 6-ship fleet was caught in a terrible storm at sea and headed to the nearest port for safety. Drake expertly navigated his ship in line with the five other English vessels into the small port town of San Juan d'Ulua on the eastern shore of New Spain (Mexico). It had a deep, beautiful harbor that safely sheltered ships from Caribbean storms. But like everything in this part of the world, the port was the property of the Spanish and they did not like to share.

They had been there only a few days when a convoy of a dozen Spanish ships desired to enter the harbor. The English had the upper hand since Hawkins' force had already taken control of the town's two batteries with its big guns protecting the harbor. The Englishmen could have easily battled the Spanish to victory.

The Spanish knew they could not enter the harbor without suffering a major defeat. They also knew that if they remained in the Caribbean, the wind and foul weather would smash them into the coral reefs. So the Spanish sent a message promising the English no harm and safe passage home if their Spanish ships were permitted to enter the harbor.

Captain John Hawkins stood before his six captains at the head of a long table in the main cabin of his fleet's 26-gun flagship, the *Jesus of Lubeck*, holding a rolled parchment between weather-beaten hands.

"The Spanish promise we can complete the repairs to our ships," said Hawkins, "and then assure us of a safe departure home."

"What choice do we have?" asked Thomas Hampton, who captained the other large Royal warship, the *Minion*. "If we attack them in their port, Queen Elizabeth will have our heads. We are not at war with Spain."

"Agreed." said Hawkins, turning to Drake. "Francis, I want you to relay the message to Viceroy Don Martin Enrique that we will abide by his request and we take his word as his bond. I want you to personally shake hands with him."

"Aye eye, Sir," replied Drake, eagerly accepting the assignment since he had never been aboard a Spanish warship.

Several days after the Spanish ships were anchored safely at port and the town's batteries returned to his command, Don Enrique double-crossed the English and smuggled 150-armed soldiers from Vera Cruz onto his two large warships late at night.

The next day to Drake's surprise he heard the sound of a Spanish trumpet float across the calm harbor waters. Immediately, musket fire rained down on the English fleet and cannon fire erupted from the shore's batteries, destroying all of Hawkins' smaller ships, except for Drake's *Judith* that luckily escaped the initial onslaught.

The English retaliated with full broadsides from the *Jesus* and the *Minion*, scoring direct hits on Don Enrique's two Spanish warships. The large Spanish merchant vessels were not a threat, but the shore's batteries riddled the *Jesus* with shot shredding her sails and masts. Hawkins' flagship was floundering and unable to flee from trouble. Hawkins signaled Hampton's *Minion* and Drake's *Judith* to hurry over and help with the removal of crew, provisions, and weapons.

In the midst of the escape, Hawkins spotted a Spanish warship, which was intentionally set on fire and set adrift, floating directly toward them. The *Minion* and *Judith*, fastened as they were to the stern of the *Jesus*, were all sitting ducks.

"Fireship!" screamed Hawkins to Hampton and Drake. "Cut the lines and get us out of here, fast!"

Drake frantically unleashed his ship from the *Jesus*. Crewmembers, who were still trying to get off the *Jesus*, jumped overboard in hopes of boarding the two departing English vessels and avoid burning to death. Very few were lucky. Drake watched in horror as his fellow Englishmen were killed when the Spanish fireship collided with the *Jesus* and exploded - killing everything in its wake.

At dusk, the big guns of San Juan d'Ulua were finally silent. The *Minion* and *Judith* were safely in the Caribbean, but struggling to prepare their overcrowded, damaged vessels for the very difficult journey home.

The year was 1568 and Drake was afraid it would be the year etched on his tombstone if he could not captain his leaky ship home. Should he survive, Drake promised himself that he would never for-

give or forget the Spanish treachery and one day he would enact his revenge.

· · ·

AFTER FOUR HORRIFYING MONTHS of enduring the extreme weather, winds, and waves while crossing the Atlantic Ocean, the overcrowded *Judith* finally arrived home at Plymouth, England. The small ship was in bad shape with torn sails, rotted wooden planks, and leaks scattered throughout the hull. The crew had plugged the leaks with strips of their own clothing, and the sailors were in even worse shape than the ship, suffering from the pains of starvation, dehydration, and severe sunburn.

Captain Drake stepped off the *Judith* feeling defeated, dishonored, and dejected. He mourned the loss of his friends in battle, his chance at returning home with treasure, and his dream of becoming a famous captain. In fact, his boyhood dream had now become a nightmare – all because of the lies of the Spanish Viceroy, Don Martin Enrique.

Looking at his wrecked ship, Drake shook his head and thought back to the days when he was a boy and first dreamed of sailing the high seas.

Francis Drake was the oldest of twelve boys. He was taught to read and write by his father, who was a preacher. When Drake was a teenager, his father found him a position as an apprentice to a skipper of a small three-masted ship that carried cargo around the Plymouth region and occasionally sailed the rough waters of the English Channel to France.

"Skipper," asked young Drake to the ship's captain as they tried to maintain the ship on course during a stormy afternoon, "I guess there is no chance of hot food on this trip, eh?"

"No," said the Skipper, pulling up the collar of his raincoat, "and you can expect many a rainy day in these seas to prevent fires from being lit and your clothes from staying dry."

"The weather does not bother me," said Drake, wiping cold rain from his brow. "My goal is to one day become a captain, like you, of my own ship."

"That is an honorable goal, son," replied the captain, fixing his rain hat snuggly on his head. "Now keep the vessel on a course of 75 degrees and be careful of the shallow shoals on our portside. The windy weather will cause the swells to drift us into these hidden dangers where many a ship have been lost."

"Aye eye, Sir," said Drake.

"As you see skippering a ship is hard work," continued the Skipper. "The sea is our home and it can be your friend one day and your foe the next, depending on your outlook and knowledge."

"Well, I will make the sea my friend," said Drake, gripping the ship's wheel with both hands to keep the vessel on course against the blustery winds, "and you can teach me the knowledge."

Several years later the Skipper passed away. He had no wife or family and since he regarded Francis as his own son, he willed his prized ship to his energetic pupil. Drake continued the business for several years and then sold the Skipper's ship. He returned home to Plymouth and searched out his older cousins, William and John Hawkins in hopes of working with them.

The Hawkins' brothers came from a family of ship owners and ran the successful business from the port of Plymouth.

"Francis, look at you!" said John Hawkins, sizing up his younger cousin by grabbing him tightly by his stocky shoulders. "You were a mere boy the last time I saw you. Now you are a strong young man."

"And a captain," said Drake, proudly. "Look at these callused hands. I now have vast experience skippering a ship to the French side of the Channel."

"I should have guessed," said Hawkins, smiling. "But we have no need for a young captain to sail our vessels to France."

"I can navigate a ship wherever you plan to go," interrupted Drake, staring into his cousin's eyes, "just give me a chance."

"Well, what do you know of the New World?" asked Hawkins, with a sly smile.

• • •

DURING THE FOUR YEARS AFTER THE DISASTROUS TRIP from Mexico with nothing to show for his efforts and no captainships available, Francis Drake took odd jobs around the docks of Portsmouth and on ships cruising the Caribbean waters to save money and develop relationships, so that one day, he could unleash his secret plan to enact revenge upon Spain's New World empire.

In 1572, Drake believed he was ready to unleash his idea. He convinced his Hawkins cousins to loan him two ships, the *Pasco* and the *Swan*. Drake recruited 70 adventurous young men like himself, purchased provisions and weapons, and hired carpenters to build three pinnaces that could be stored in pieces. Pinnaces were small vessels propelled by mainsails and oars and used for sailing inland waterways. They were vital to Drake's cloak-and-dagger plan that he discussed with nobody but his cousins.

Drake planned to raid the Spanish where they least expected it. He had learned from sailors along his travels that the gold, silver, and precious jewels from Peru and Chile were shipped northwards to the city of Panama on the Pacific side of the Isthmus of Darien. There, a convoy of pack-mules transported the treasure across land to the town of Nombre de Dios on the Caribbean side of the isthmus. Here, this amazing wealth was stored at what was referred to as the "treasure house of the world" protected by a garrison of armed guards until a fleet of large Spanish treasure galleons arrived from Spain to pick it up and carry it across the Atlantic Ocean to King Philip II.

Drake anchored his two ships in a secluded bay north of Nombre de Dios and had his crew assemble the three pinnaces for a sneak attack from the Chagres River. On the journey along the banks of the winding river, Drake made friends with tribes of cimarrones giving them gifts of pottery and pewter bowls. Cimarrones were Negro outlaws who escaped Spanish slavery and banded together in the dangerous jungles of Panama. They had one thing in common with Drake – they hated the Spanish as much as him! One cimarrone named Diego was especially helpful and lead Drake's expedition on foot for days through the dense jungle until they reached the exact path that the treasure mule train traveled from Panama to Nombre de Dios.

At one point during the hot, bug-infested journey, Diego walked Drake and his second-in-command, John Oxenham, up a high hill to a very large tree. The cimarrones had cut steps into the trunk of the tree for easy climbing to a tree stand they had built. Standing at the top of the tree, Drake looked to the east and saw the familiar Caribbean Sea. But for the first time in any Englishman's life, when Drake looked to the west he witnessed the mighty Pacific Ocean.

"Diego," said Drake, "One day I will sail in those Spanish waters."

"Be careful, Captain," replied Diego, wiping his sweaty black brow, "If they catch you, they will torture you to death."

"They must catch me first," said Drake, smiling while patting his new friend on the shoulder.

"Look!" said Oxenham, excitedly, staring through the spyglass. "I can see the mule train making its way out of Panama. There are hundreds of them!"

"Hurry and assemble the crew," said Drake. "I have an idea."

Instead of raiding the heavily guarded town of Nombre de Dios, Drake changed his attack strategy.

"Oxenham," said Drake, "Take half our men and the cimarrones and head down the path a league. Spread the company out on either side of the path and hide in the jungle bush. Allow the entire mule train to pass and when the last mule passes your position, fire a warning shot, and then attack from the rear."

"Yes, Sir!" replied Oxenham, excitedly. "I will prevent any treasure mules from retreating to Panama."

"Go now!" said Drake, "And make sure your men know to stay hidden until you fire the shot."

Drake's men waited patiently for what seemed like hours, crouched in the dense jungle, swatting away mosquitoes and being careful to avoid poisonous snakes. Suddenly, the sound of mule bells was heard through the still forest, followed by the hooves of the animals stomping on the hard ground. There were nearly two hundred mules, each carrying a wooden chest or leather saddlebags, plodding their way along the well-worn path under an escort of fifty armed Spanish soldiers. Finally, when the last mule in the train passed Oxenham's hiding spot, he fired a loud shot into the air.

"Charge!" cried Drake when he heard the gunshot.

He quickly appeared with his sword raised, surprising the two guards on horseback who were leading the mule train. At the same time, Drake's force left their hiding places and surrounded the Spanish guards around the entire length of the treasure train.

"Drop your weapons!" said Diego in Spanish to the shocked guard holding the reins of the lead mule. All of the guards, seeing they were surrounded at gunpoint, instantly raised their arms in the air and surrendered.

"Make your mule lie down on the ground," Diego commanded. Diego knew that the trained mules would all follow the lead of the first mule, which would prevent them from running scared into the jungle.

"Good work, Diego," said Drake, as he picked up the guard's weapon and watched him nudge the mule to the ground.

Drake held the Spanish guards at gunpoint and removed the chest from the lead mule's back. He then used the butt of the guard's musket to smash open the lid. He could not believe his blue eyes. The chest was filled to the top with gold pesos or doubloons.

Drake's pirate crew were hooting and hollering as they plundered the contents of the mule train. They had never seen riches like this before in their entire lives.

"Look what I found," said Oxenham, walking up to Drake with a beautiful gold necklace with a large silver cross covered in jewels hanging from his neck and emerald rings sparkling on his fingers.

"John," said Drake, laughing at Oxenham's royal appearance, "have the men carry as much treasure as they can hold. We must get out of here! The troops at Nombre de Dios will come searching for us as soon as the treasure train doesn't arrive on time."

"Aye eye, captain," said Oxenham, "they will most likely send warships to scour the Caribbean coastline to cut off our retreat as well."

Drake turned his attention to Diego. "Diego, I need you to guide us back to the ships as quickly as possible."

"Captain, we must go back the way we came," said Diego, pointing into the bush. "What do you want to do with the guards? Kill them?

"No," answered Drake, "put them to work carrying the chests."

"But there's too much coin to carry, captain," replied Oxenham, staring at the countless number of treasure containers – chests and saddlebags - scattered along the mule path.

"Bury it!" commanded Drake. "What we cannot carry, we will come back to get later."

Diego led Drake's force and the prisoners back into the jungle on foot for the return trip to the pinnaces. The men had to move as quickly as possible because they were only hours ahead of a large force of Spanish soldiers, who were immediately dispatched when mules walked into the town of Nombre de Dios without escorts and without the gold and silver. Drake's crew knew that if they were captured, there would be no treasure, no trial, only torture!

The days were hot and long and the men were weary from the long, horrible hike carrying the heavy treasure and their weapons. Drake would not permit them to rest for fear of being caught. Finally, after two full days, they reached the pinnaces where everything was stored securely in place. The crew rowed sluggishly up river to where they had anchored the two ships.

Once safely aboard the *Pasco* with the ship's hold filled with treasure, Drake freed the Spanish prisoners and awarded gifts to the cimarrones for their help, including the pinnaces and a number of crossbows. The natives were overjoyed since they had no need for treasure in the jungle.

Now, with the tide rising, it was time to shove off for the last leg of Drake's first successful expedition. But danger still loomed in the distance as Drake's ships had to escape the Spanish warships waiting for him in the Caribbean Sea.

• • •

SEVERAL MONTHS LATER, a big sweaty dockworker was pointing out to the Plymouth Sound and asked, "What's that Spanish ship doing in our waters?"

"Well, the ship might be Spanish made," said his co-worker, who looked intently at the strange vessel, "but she's flying English colors and red privateer banners."

"Do you think it might be Drake?" asked another, shielding the sun's glare from his eyes.

When the word "Drake" floated across the salty dockyard air, workers dropped their crates, stopped stacking barrels, and turned their attention instead to the Spanish galleon heading their way.

"Drake is dead," shouted a worker over the excited mumblings of the gathering crowd. "He's been gone for over a year. And I heard he was captured and the Spanish Inquisition tortured him to death."

"Well then, it must be his ghost," said the dockworker who first spotted the vessel, "because that short, red-headed chap at the bow of the ship sure looks like my old friend Francis Drake!"

Immediately, people started shouting and running through the streets to spread the thrilling news that Drake had finally returned home after a year at sea. Merchants, sailors, farmers, and fami-

lies from all over town quickly drifted to the docks to see the strange vessel maneuver into a slip.

The crowd burst into applause when Drake, accompanied by John Oxenham and a large black man, appeared at the gunwale playfully displaying handfuls of gold, silver, and sparkling jewelry for everyone to see.

The crowd went crazy with excitement! They were cheering, applauding and dancing!

"Francis, welcome home," said his cousin John Hawkins.

Hawkins was the first to walk up the gangplank, followed by his favorite nephew Oscar, to greet their kinfolk, now the town's conquering hero.

"I thought I would never see you or my ships again," Hawkins said.

After a firm affectionate hug, he asked, "By the way, where are my ships?"

"I'm sorry, Cousin," replied Drake, "We lost the *Swan* and several of the crew in a terrible tropical storm. The *Pasco* was a good fighting ship, but she took too many blows below the water line during our battle with this here Spanish beauty." He stomped his foot on the deck of the ship.

"What happened?" asked Hawkins, as he paced the deck inspecting the ship's beautiful woodwork.

"Just after we weighed anchor at a latitude just north of Nombre de Dios, we were surprised by the Spanish," said Drake. "We blasted one of King Philip's ships, but took a devastating broadside. Luckily, I had the weather gage so I crashed the *Pasco* into her amidships and we boarded this Spanish galleon with gusto!"

"I wish I was with you," said Hawkins with pride and not a little envy as he continued inspecting the ornate gold carvings of the quarterdeck.

"John," said Drake, shrewdly, "I hope she will be a suitable replacement for your two ships lost on my watch."

"Oh, yes indeed!" replied Hawkins, smiling and hugging his cousin once again. It was then that he noticed Drake's crew coming from the hold carrying chests and bags onto the main deck. "Do all of these chests contain treasure?"

"Ha!" laughed Drake, as he opened one of the wooden chests filled to the brim with shining gold coins. "Yes, the Spanish were nice enough to share their New World wealth with us."

"Holy Mother of England!" exclaimed Hawkins in admiration. "Our dear Queen Elizabeth will be your best friend when her eyes alight on this plunder."

"Uncle Francis," asked young Oscar, inspecting a handful of gold doubloons, "where did you get all of this gold?"

"We borrowed it from the Spanish...for keeps!" said Drake, laughing aloud.

"Amazing!" said Oscar. "Can I have one coin?"

"No, Oscar," replied Drake, laughing, "We must account for every piece of this treasure. Maybe your uncle will give you one from his share for lending his ships to me."

"Utterly astounding!" exclaimed Hawkins, smiling from ear to ear. "But how did you know of the mule train?"

"Diego!" said Drake, calling the black man away from his work stacking the chests. "This man and his tribe showed us the secret path the Spanish use to transport the treasure from Panama to Nombre de Dios. They assisted in our ambush plans and lead us through the bush and back to our pinnaces."

"Is he your slave now?" asked Oscar, looking at the muscular black man with the tribal tattoos.

"No, Oscar. He chose to stay and sail with me. And now he is my right hand man."

"Uncle Francis," asked the inquisitive Oscar, "can I sail with you?"

"Yes, Oscar. Yes, you can one day," said Drake with a sparkle in his eye. "But be prepared to sail where no Englishman has ever sailed before."

• • •

ON NOVEMBER 15TH, 1577, four years after Francis Drake's return from plundering the Spanish treasure mule train, he set sail on his newly built ship, the 18-gun *Pelican*, with a crew of 80, including Diego as his trusted servant and Oscar as his personal page. Four smaller vessels, the *Elizabeth*, *Marigold*, *Benedict*, and *Swan*, accompanied his flagship on this clandestine voyage.

Drake's pirate flotilla sailed south along the African Coast. Off the Cape Verdes Islands, he captured a Portuguese ship named the *Santa Maria*. In addition to yielding a large supply of provisions, like barrels of salted meat and fresh fruit, the prize had a navigator, Nuno da Silva, who owned hand-

drawn nautical charts and had vast experience navigating South America's waters.

Drake forced Nuno to sail on the *Pelican* as his pilot since no Englishman knew the waters they were about to navigate. Drake renamed the *Santa Maria* after his wife Mary. And the *Mary* became his sixth ship, continuing on to their secret destination.

The night before the fleet would try to cross the dreaded Strait of Magellan at the southernmost tip of South America, Drake convened a council of captains at Port San Julian aboard his flagship, renamed the *Golden Hind*.

"Gentlemen," said Drake, "the most treacherous portion of the journey is before us. The Strait has the most dangerous waters in the world."

"Only one man in the world has successfully navigated this route," added John Winter, Drake's second-in-command and the captain of the *Elizabeth*. "His name was Ferdinand Magellan and they named the waterway after him."

"So, you see what you're up against," continued Drake. "I want your crews to have a full night's rest and make sure your ships are fully fit for sail."

"Captain Drake," said John Thomas, the captain of the *Marigold*, hesitantly, "Are you sure this is wise? We are not even sure what we will find, should we even make it to the other side of the passage."

"I will tell you again what we will find," declared Drake, raising his voice. "The South Seas is King Philip's lake and it is filled with his ships shuttling treasure up the coast to Panama. And it is ripe for the raiding! They will not expect Englishmen in their backyard!"

"But we are not at war with Spain," said Francis Fletcher, the captain of the *Mary*, sharing Captain Thomas's concern. "We will be hung as pirates if we are caught."

"That is a more pleasant death than what the Spanish Inquisition would do to you," said Diego, standing behind Drake's captain chair. "Captain Drake has the most to fear since the King of Spain has placed a price upon his head after raiding his treasure at Nombre de Dios."

After two terrible weeks of relentless westerly winds, fog, and mountainous seas, the *Golden Hind* finally arrived in the South Sea. But she was alone. The *Elizabeth* had abandoned the voyage and returned to England. And she was luckier than the rest of the fleet, which was lost when gale-size

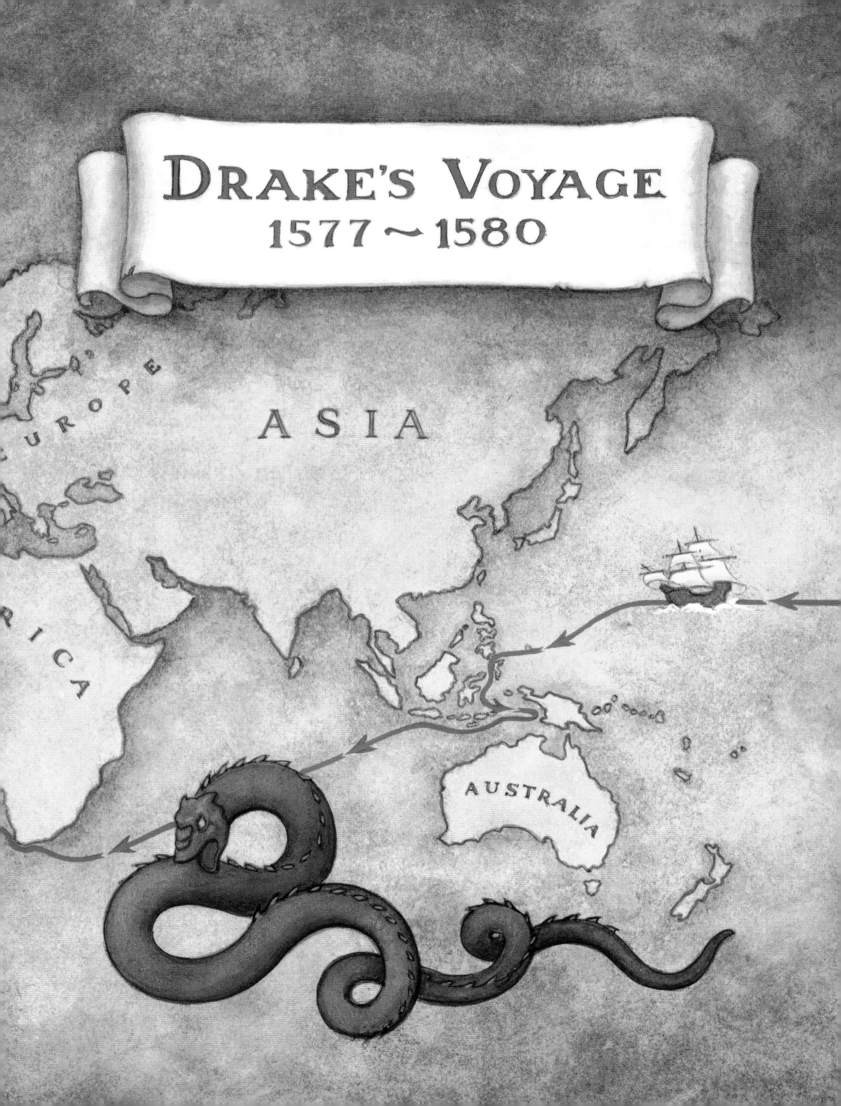

waves washed them into the large rocks that jutted up throughout the Strait.

Drake plundered several unsuspecting Spanish vessels and raided ports as he forged north along the Pacific coast in search of the king's treasure galleons. On more than one occasion, Drake used punishing measures to uncover information from his prisoners. He persuaded one Spanish captain—by tying a rope around his waist and dunking him overboard—to disclose that one of the most prized ships lay just a day ahead of him. Drake offered a gold chain to whoever saw the treasure ship.

"Sail ho!" screamed Oscar from the crow's nest, pointing at a sail on the horizon.

Drake peered through spyglass and focused in the direction of Oscar's arm. He saw the name of *Nuestra Señora de la Concepcion* on her stern.

"Yes!" said Drake, excitedly. "We have our Queen's fortune in sight." And then he yelled up the mainmast, "Oscar, you are my good luck charm!"

The *Golden Hind* launched a fully armed pinnace to attack the port side of the *Concepcion* while she sailed to her other flank to surround the prey.

"Englishmen," yelled the trumpeter on the *Golden Hind* to the Spanish galleon, "Strike sail!"

When the Spanish flag was not readily hauled down, the trumpeter blew the attack, and cannon and musket fire bombarded the treasure ship. The pinnace tossed grappling hooks and the crew scrabbled up and over the gunwales. The Spanish immediately surrendered. They never expected to be attacked in their waters and were not prepared for the wild, weapon-wielding marauders.

Drake boarded the *Concepcion*, hoisted the flag portraying the red St. George Cross, and had the ship's captain brought to the main deck.

"Captain San Juan de Anton," said Drake, dramatically, "your ship and all of her contents are now the property of Queen Elizabeth the Great!"

"The King will see you hanged for this offense," said Anton. "We are not at war with England."

"Spain was not at war with England a decade ago when you murdered our crew and sunk our ships at San Juan d'Ulua," said Drake with a vengeance in his voice. "I will make your country pay and pay and pay for the loss of my friends."

"Captain," interrupted Lieutenant Tom Moone, holding a bound leather journal, "we have found

the manifest that shows the amount of registered treasure aboard ship."

"What does it read?" asked Drake.

"There appears to be chests that contain 360,000 silver pesos, 80 pounds of gold, and 26 tons of silver bars," replied Moone, raising his eyes in amazement.

"Wonderful!" exclaimed Drake. "Get the men to ferry the treasure to the *Golden Hind*. And be sure to search the ship for all the gold and silver smuggled aboard that may not be listed on the manifest. These thieving Spanish will steal from their own king."

Drake turned his attention back to the Spanish captain with a sly smile, thinking of King Philip's reaction to losing his treasure to the redheaded Englishman.

Once the *Golden Hind* was beached, careened and cleaned of barnacles, filled with new provisions from the *Concepcion*, and its hold packed with treasure, Drake set off for the dangerous voyage home. But he could not return the route he came.

The Spanish would be waiting for him with fully armed vessels seeking revenge. They did not believe he would risk traveling across the untamed Pacific Ocean and were making plans to finally capture "El Draque" (the Dragon), as he was now called.

Ever since Drake's outrageous mule train robbery at Nombre de Dios, King Phillip sent out word across the Caribbean that he wanted this pirate El Draque brought to him dead or alive. The king wanted to make an example of Drake and show the world what happens to anyone who invades his Spanish empire.

Francis Drake and his crew of the *Golden Hind* did not return the way they had come; but instead, continued north to the latitude of San Francisco where he set a westward course just above the Equator. Despite uncharted waters, blazing sunshine, hurricane-like storms, tribal uprisings, mysterious island reefs, and battling scurvy, dehydration and starvation, Drake's courage, leadership, and seamanship enabled his little 70-foot ship to journey across the vast Pacific Ocean, through the Palau and Spice Islands, span the Indian Ocean, and sail down and around the Cape of Good Hope, the southernmost tip of Africa. Finally, they headed north in the Atlantic Ocean, hugging the Guinea Coast of Africa to the familiar surroundings of the Canary Islands.

After almost three years and sailing all the way around the world, Drake was almost home with more treasure than any Englishman had ever plundered before him. And he had traveled where no Englishman had ever been before him. But he had dreadful concerns: Was Queen Elizabeth still in power? Could the King of Spain demand his arrest? Would the treasure be confiscated and returned to Spain? Would he be hung as a pirate?

• • •

AFTER COVERTLY OFFLOADING A CHEST of treasure at a remote location, Drake maneuvered the *Golden Hind* into the English Channel toward his beloved homeport in Plymouth Sound. He was concerned a welcoming party in England might have a hangman's rope waiting for him instead of a laurel wreath, so he tasked Oscar to flag down the first vessel he saw.

"Sailor!" called Oscar to a small two-man fishing boat, "is Queen Elizabeth still alive?"

"Of course," replied the sailor, confused by the odd question. "From whence have you sailed?"

"Around the world!" shouted Oscar, relieved to hear the Queen was still on the throne.

"You are a wise-arse, boy." Then the other fisherman asked sarcastically, "I suppose next you will tell us that your captain is none other than the sea dog Francis Drake?"

"He will. And he would be correct!" called Drake, leaning on the gunwale and placing his arm around Oscar's shoulders, stunning the sailors at the sight of the infamous captain dressed in a full suit of armor.

"God bless you, Captain Drake," said the fisherman. "News is the Spanish call you a pirate, but we, English, call you hero."

Drake was well aware that his pirating of Portuguese and Spanish ships and settlements would not go unpunished by anyone but his queen. He knew that Queen Elizabeth did not publicly support his expeditions against the Spanish, but she did welcome any treasure he stole from that bully King Phillip. So just in case his monarch might have died, Drake had devised an alternate plan. Trailing directly behind the *Golden Hind* was a pinnace stocked with provisions, weapons, and a few faithful crewmembers to aid in his escape and return to where he had hidden some of the treasure.

But on September 15, 1580, Drake anchored the *Golden Hind* at Plymouth. He did not disembark

because one of the fishermen notified him that the city was infected with the plague. Instead, his wife Mary Drake and the Mayor of Plymouth, John Blitheman, were rowed out to the *Golden Hind* to welcome Drake home and share the latest gossip circulating across England.

"Francis, I am told that the Queen wants to meet you!" said Mary, enthusiastically, after they affectionately hugged and the initial hellos were completed. Then she looked around and asked, "Is it true this ship is filled with treasure?"

"Yes, my dear," replied Drake, proudly, "our voyage was a stunning success and our lives will be changed forever."

"Hopefully for the better, Captain Drake," said the Mayor, cautiously. "The Spanish Ambassador wants you arrested and the treasure returned to its rightful owner. "

"In that case," smiled Drake, "I should return it to the Inca natives in South America from whom the Spanish stole it."

"I do not jest," said the Mayor, concerned that Drake did not appreciate the severity of the situation. "Word out of London is that King Philip is building an armada to make war with England if the treasure is not returned."

"The King of Spain will make war with every nation that does not agree with his ways," said Drake. "He is a tyrant who wants to rule the world and one day he will push us Englishmen too far."

"Enough about war, Francis," said Mary, anxiously, "please show me the treasure."

• • •

SEVERAL WEEKS LATER, DRAKE TRAVELED to London by horseback and was ushered into the private chambers of Queen Elizabeth. There he shared his extraordinary tales of adventure. He showed her his hand-drawn charts of lands in the New World claimed under her name. He described the hunt for the treasure galleon *Nuestra Senora de la Concepcion*. And concluded his amazing account by slowly opening a large leather pouch, from which he poured an assortment of gold, silver, and gems into her ring-studded hands.

"Captain Drake," said the Queen, staring at the glittering gems, "we are very proud of you and your circumnavigation of the world. It is truly unbelievable!"

"Thank you, Your Majesty," replied Drake, humbly. "May I ask a question?"

"Speak."

"Must this treasure be returned to the King of Spain?" asked Drake, who also wondered about his own prospects of incarceration—or worse.

"Philip can raise his voice and threaten the Monarchy," said the Queen, "but by the blood of my father, King Henry VIII, I will not see him receive one silver coin from your conquest."

She lowered her voice and leaned forward, "I want you to remove £10,000 for yourself before you transport the treasure to the Tower of London to be registered and stored for safekeeping. Do not worry, Captain Drake, the Spanish will not force me to imprison my pirate in the Tower with England's treasure."

In the 16th century, £10,000 was a fortune and Drake was both warmed and relieved by the Queen's favor. He smiled the largest smile of his adventurous 40-year life, then knelt on one knee and kissed the Queen's ring.

The incredible exploits of Drake spread far and wide and he was swarmed by ordinary English folk wherever he appeared. He was not born of the privileged nobility; he was one of the commoners. He never lost the common touch and treated everyone with respect.

On April 1st, 1581, when the *Golden Hind* sat proudly in dry dock in Deptford, England, the entire population of London turned out to see Queen Elizabeth board the fabled ship, accompanied by the French Ambassador, Monsieur de Marchaumont. The immense throng of common folk wanted to celebrate the impossibility that one of their own would be transformed into knighthood. It was an incredible occasion.

Kneeling before Queen Elizabeth, Drake watched her hand the bejeweled sword to Marchaumont to conduct the ceremony, cunningly involving the nation of France in her bold act of rebelliousness against King Philip of Spain – and his intimidating threat of war.

• • •

SIR FRANCIS DRAKE was now a man of honor and wealth. He had a knight's title with a beautiful coat of arms granted by the Queen of England. He purchased the estate of Buckland Abbey to the north of Plymouth as his country house with his portion of the plunder from the *Concepcion*. He served as Mayor of Plymouth and a Member of Parliament. He remarried a beautiful heiress, Elizabeth Sydenham, after the death of his beloved wife. He was a national hero to his countrymen and adored by the rich and poor alike.

But none of these personal treasures calmed Drake's restless energy, determination, and merciless spirit to bring down the King of Spain.

Luckily for Drake, Queen Elizabeth discovered in 1585 that her arch-nemesis, King Philip, was building a vast armada to make war with England - and had declared an embargo on English vessels.

"Sir Francis," said Queen Elizabeth, who had summoned Drake to London, "it has come to my attention that the London merchant ship *Primrose* has docked with horrible news."

"What is it, Your Majesty?" asked Drake, concerned about his Queen's distress.

"The *Primrose* was boarded in the Spanish Bay of Bilboa," replied the Queen, "but she fought free and escaped. During the fight, her captain retrieved this document from the invaders that shows clear and concise instructions from King Philip to his Spanish officials to seize all English ships."

"This is an act of war!" exclaimed Drake, staring at the Spanish document in the Queen's small hands. "That scoundrel is confiscating our ships and artillery to add to his Armada to use against us! We must strike first and strike hard!"

"Calm down, Sir Francis," said the Queen, secretly enjoying her pirate's temper. "I will not start a war even though you hope I do. But I do authorize you to raise a fleet and visit the ports of the Spanish empire to release all impounded English ships and crews."

The Queen leaned forward. "I also want you to recoup any financial losses anyway you see fit," she added in a low conspiratorial whisper and a wink of her left eye.

"With pleasure, Your Majesty," said a smiling Drake. His Queen had just given him permission to sail for the first time under the flag of St. George as a "privateer" and plunder Spanish possessions. A privateer, unlike a pirate, is sanctioned by the government with a legal Letter of Marque, entitling him to battle enemies against the Crown and to keep a percentage of the booty.

In 1585, Admiral Drake assembled a fleet of 25 ships, including two naval vessels contributed by the Queen. Drake took one of the ships, the *Elizabeth Bonaventure*, as his flagship. He appointed Thomas Fenner as her captain and Oscar as one of her lieutenants.

Many of Drake's loyal men who had accompanied him on previous voyages were made ship captains within the fleet. Drake named Christopher Carleill Lieutenant General of the expedition and appointed him commander of 12 companies of soldiers - the majority of his two thousand men. Drake planned to raid by land and by sea.

The first stop of the English fleet was at the town of Vigo in northwestern Spain where Drake walked onto Spanish soil for the first time in his life and brazenly questioned the local governor.

What Drake really wanted to do was storm the king's castle in Seville to repay the King personally for the incident at San Juan d'Ulua almost 20 years earlier. Drake never forgot the humiliating battle and the treachery of the Spanish, which continually fueled the burning desire in his belly to make war with Spain.

But, standing before Vigo's governor, Drake calmed his long festering anger.

"Don Pedro Bermudez," said Drake, who was accompanied by Carleill, "I want to ask you two questions."

"Yes, Admiral Drake," said Bermudez, fearing for his life and the safety of his town as he stood before the most dreaded of Englishmen and the powerful fleet at his command. "I am at your mercy."

The governor, like every Spaniard on the planet, heard of the terrifying exploits of the pirate Drake. Rumors spread far and wide of him burning towns to the ground, robbing treasure, boarding ships, taking hostages, and cutting throats. Children, who misbehaved, were threatened by their parents that El Draque would visit them in the middle of the night.

"Is Spain at war with England?" asked Drake, resting his hand on his sword and using his scary reputation as a threat.

"No, Señor," replied Bermudez, shaking his head vigorously.

"Why then did your king impound our ships?" asked Drake, removing his sword from its scabbard.

"Señor, it was a misunderstanding," said Bermudez, with perspiration dotting his worried brow. "The English ships have been released to my knowledge."

"We shall see," said Drake, drawing an "X" in the sand with his sword. "And while we are here, we will provision our vessels."

"Claro que sí, Señor," the governor readily replied. Of course. Bermudez wanted to appease Drake and prevent the ruin of his town.

King Philip was livid—and worried—when he heard that Drake had been on Spanish soil demanding provisions. He immediately sent out dispatches to his holdings in the West Indies and New World that "El Draque" was on the loose.

The city of Santiago in Cape Verdes was the first to hear the cry "God and St. George" when it was attacked by Drake's guns from the harbor and by a coordinated rear attack by Carleill's land force. The town was stripped of all artillery, valuables, and food, and held for a handsome ransom.

Santo Domingo, the oldest Spanish city in the New World in southeastern Hispaniola, was next to suffer the effects of Drake's brilliant battle strategy. Drake instituted a fierce naval bombardment off of the port to distract the city's defenses, while an assault force moved into position to launch a surprise attack from on land.

The flag of St. George would flap in the wind above the conquered city until Drake's ransom demands were met. He would make sure of it.

The treasure port of Cartagena on the Spanish Main fared no better. Though the Spanish troops fought bravely, they fell under Drake's land-and-sea assault. The capture of this famous city sent shockwaves rippling across the Caribbean; it demonstrated to the world that King Philip's empire was more vulnerable than previously thought and that no Spanish port was safe from Drake's violent vengeance.

Drake wanted to raid Havana, Cuba, before the expedition turned homeward, but the weather and winds prevented safe anchorage. Instead, his fleet sailed the Straits of Florida, hugging the eastern coast, where a lookout spotted a watchtower on a small island bordered by an inlet. The location marked St. Augustine, the most northerly town in Spain's overseas empire.

Drake sent a landing party to investigate the deserted watchtower while Carleill lead a force to the opposite side of the inlet. On the night of May 28th, 1586, Indians allied with the Spanish launched a surprise night assault on the English camp. Drake and his men held their ground and counterattacked, now with renewed vigor sparked by the bold attack.

The following morning, a very angry Drake unleashed his 2000-strong force on the wooden fort and town, burning everything to the ground. The English recovered 14 bronze cannons and over 2,000 gold ducats that were left behind when the army garrison and settlers quickly fled inland for safety. Then, Drake and his men took to the sea once again.

After almost a year at sea, Drake's great expedition sailed into Plymouth to the cheers of a colossal crowd lining the wharf. But the fleet would not have much time to rest, repair, and enjoy the spoils of Drake's personal war with Spain because it was soon to become England's war.

• • •

"SIR FRANCIS," said Queen Elizabeth, losing patience with her favorite swashbuckling seaman, "we cannot afford to spend more money on ships and men so you can fight a war with Spain!"

"I am sorry, Your Majesty," Drake pleaded, "but King Philip's Armada is growing stronger as we speak. We must conduct a pre-emptive strike before he brings a war to us."

"Sir Howard," said the Queen, directing her attention to her Lord Admiral, "what are the latest reports from the Iberian Peninsula?"

"Your Majesty," replied Sir Howard of Effingham, "Sir Francis is correct. We have evidence of ships and supplies mobilizing throughout the ports of Spain."

But to remain in his Queen's good graces, Sir Howard suggested: "Why not send out just an exploratory force to see for ourselves?"

"And if the Armada has sailed from Spain," added Drake, sensing an opportunity to set sail, "we can slow her down and signal for fleet reinforcements before she reaches England."

"By St. George's sword, Sir Francis," said the Queen, shaking her head in mock annoyance, "you will be the death of me."

With a fleet of 24 ships, Drake paroled south along the Spanish coast, taking several Spanish prizes along the way to his desired destination, Cadiz, where he believed the dreaded Armada was gathering. The Queen and Lord Admiral granted him orders to engage if he saw the Armada. They did not say "at sea only."

Emboldened by their leader's courage and daring, Drake's fleet sailed directly into the port of Cadiz without flying flags or pennants; they passed the cannon-laden batteries as if they belonged in these waters. By the time the Spanish recognized the vessels as English, it was too late.

The Queen's ships raised their colors, sounded their trumpets, and unleashed Drake's wrath. None of the 60 vessels in port - including war galleys, galleons, armed merchantmen, and Armada storeships - were spared the fury and marksmanship of the English warships.

Drake's destruction of the port of Cadiz showed that none of King Philip's cities and fleets were free from the dagger of El Draque. In addition to delaying the launch of the Spanish Armada by a year, the attack also inflicted psychological damage on Spain and provided a tremendous morale boost for England.

During the spring of 1588, Lord Admiral Howard held a council of war with his top advisors aboard his flagship *Ark Royal*, in preparation for the looming war with Spain's terrifying Armada.

"Dispatches notify us," said an alarmed John Hawkins, the fleet's Rear-Admiral, "that the Armada looks to be leaving Lisbon with a 150 ships and a force of almost 30,000 men!"

"All the more reason to set sail immediately and intercept them before they enter the English

Channel!" said Drake, the feet's Vice-Admiral and now his cousin's superior.

"How many vessels do we have provisioned in Plymouth?" asked Lord Admiral Howard.

"Half as many as Spain," replied Hawkins. "But our ships are faster, lighter, and we can mount more broadside guns thanks to our new ship design."

"Good," said Howard. "We certainly cannot allow them close quarters so they can board us. Their ships are too big and their numbers too great."

"I will have the 40 guns on my flagship *Revenge* blasting as I run circles around Philip's bloated seahorses," said Drake, as he anxiously paced the room like an attack dog on a dangerously short leash.

"Gentlemen, I will discuss with the Queen," said Howard, calling the meeting to a close. "And I suggest you have plenty of powder and shot aboard your ships."

The English were unable to prevent Spain's great fleet from entering their waters. And now, before them lay the amazing Armada, extending for over two miles in battle formation—a breath away from English soil.

Howard divided the English fleet into squadrons. He ordered Drake's fleet to sail around the Armada and begin an assault from the Spanish rear. Drake's courage, seamanship, and experience – and his childhood knowledge of the local waters – helped him navigate the volatile currents and dangerous shoals to position himself perfectly to take the wind out of Spanish sails.

With precision cannon fire and expert navigation, Drake's squadron destroyed, captured, and ran aground many of the Spanish vessels. The squadrons of Howard and Hawkins, assisted by God's winds, weather, and tides, prevented the Spanish Armada from landfall at England's Isle of Wright and forced her further into the hazardous currents of the North Sea toward Scotland. The Armada limped north through the rough seas without a safe port to repair her battle- and sea-worn vessels, all because the indefatigable Drake was snapping at her bloodied heels.

• • •

THE ARMADA WAS DEFEATED. England was protected against invasion from the most powerful empire in the world. But Drake's vendetta against Spain and King Philip continued until his dying breath.

The seaman, politician, privateer, husband, entrepreneur, circumnavigator, explorer, and pirate remained restless until his final voyage to the West Indies in 1595 in hopes of plundering Panama. But in January of the following year, aboard his flagship *Defiance*, near the entrance to Puerto Bello, Drake died from dysentery.

On January 28th, 1596, the body of Sir Francis Drake - the sailor from humble beginnings who became a knight, the first Englishman to navigate around the world, the warrior who singlehandedly wrecked havoc and fear on Spain's New World empire - was dressed in full armor and encased in a coffin lined with lead and slowly lowered into the Caribbean Sea to the sound of trumpets and the thunder of the fleet's guns as his crew paid their last respects to England's greatest naval hero.

Glossary of Terms

Amidships - midway between the bow and stern of a ship.

Armada – the Spanish fleet that sailed against England.

Articles of Piracy – a set of rules or pirate code that every crewmember was expected to follow while aboard ship. By signing the articles, a pirate was ensured that he had an equal vote regarding the management of the ship, distribution of booty, and punishment should the code be broken.

Battery - a unit of cannon staged to protect a port from attack.

Barque – a three-masted ship with a deep hold for carrying cargo.

Bow - front end of a boat.

Broadside - the simultaneous firing of the cannon along one side of a ship.

Cimarrone - escaped Spanish slave who lived in the jungle and raided Spanish settlements.

Circumnavigation - traveling all the way around.

Close quarters - very short distance between ships.

Convoy - a group of boats and/or ships traveling together.

Cutlass – a slightly curved short sword used in close-quarters fighting. Unlike the longer sword, a cutlass would not get caught in the rigging when boarding an enemy ship.

Dagger – a small blade about six inches or less used in close-quarters combat.

Doubloon – a very valuable gold coin weighing approximately one ounce and worth 16 pieces of eight.

English Channel - narrow extension of the Atlantic Ocean separating the southern coast of England from the northern coast of France.

Flagship - the ship used by the commanding officer of a group of naval vessels.

Flotilla - a formation of small warships.

Fireship – an abandoned vessel filled with black powder, pitch, tar, and sulfur and then lit on fire. The floating bomb is sailed directly into an enemy ship.

Galleon - a large, multi-deck ship powered by sails carried on three or four masts.

Gangplank - a board used as a temporary bridge between a ship and the dock.

Grappling hook - a device with multiple hooks or claws and attached to a rope to be flung over a ship's gunwales to aid in boarding the prey.

Gunwales - top edge of the side of a boat.

Latitude - a geographic coordinate that specifies the north-south location on the earth's surface.

League - the equivalent to 3 nautical miles.

Letter of Marque – a license from the government granting a person the right to plunder enemy possessions.

Isthmus of Darien - narrow strip of land that lies between the Caribbean Sea and the Pacific Ocean.

Merchantman - a merchant ship carrying goods.

Musket - a long barreled gun fired from the shoulder.

Pieces of eight – Spanish silver coins that weighed approximately one ounce and contained a very high quality of silver. Pirates would often cut the coin with their sword or dagger into eight pieces or bits to make smaller currency.

Pinnace - small vessel propelled by a main sail and oars used for sailing inland waterways.

Pirate – a person who robs at sea or plunders the land from sea without authority from the government.

Port - left side of a ship.

Powder monkey – a young teenage boy who carried bags of gunpowder from the powder magazine in the ship's hold to the gun crews during battle.

Privateer – a private person or ship with permission from their monarch (letter of marque) to attack and capture enemy nations' ships during wartime.

Queen Elizabeth - reigned over England from 1558 to 1603.

Sea dog - sailor

Scurvy - a disease common among sailors due to ad efficiency of vitamin C found in citrus fruits.

Spanish Inquisition - the Spanish tortured and persecuted people and enemies who did not share in their same religious beliefs.

Starboard - right side of a ship.

Stern - back end of a boat.

Tower of London – a prison castle on the banks of the River Thames in London, England.

Weather gage - where one ship is upwind of another and can either initiate attack or break off and run.

Bibliographies
. . . .

Andrews, Kenneth R., Editor. The Last Voyage of Drake and Hawkins. Cambridge: Cambridge University Press, 1972.

Cordingly, David. Under the Black Flag. Orlando: Harcourt Brace & Company, 1995.

Konstam, Angus. Pirates - Predators of the Seas. New York: Skyhorse Publishing, 2007.

Marx, Jenifer. Pirates and Privateers of the Caribbean. Malabar: Krieger Publishing Co., 1992.

Maynard, Tho. Voyage of Sir Fr Drake. Captain's journal located in The British Library, 1596.

Parker, Derek. The Queen's Pirates. London: Scholastic Books, 2004.

Sugden, John. Sir Francis Drake. New York: Simon & Schuster, 1990.